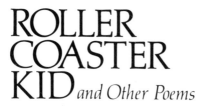

ROLLER COASTER KID *and Other Poems*

Love, Beastly Love

CHA CHA CHA

1/11

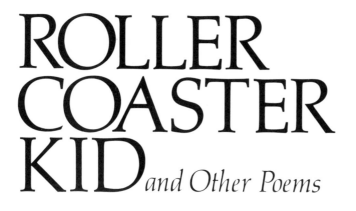

ROLLER COASTER KID *and Other Poems*

by Barry Wallenstein

Thomas Y. Crowell   New York

"Roller Coaster Kid" appeared in slightly altered form in *Observation Post;* "Deception" appeared in *Centennial Review* and *Beast Is a Wolf with Brown Fire;* "Spider's Way" appeared in *Beast Is a Wolf with Brown Fire;* "Fantastic" appeared in slightly altered form in *Open Places.* The quotation used in the discussion of "The Careful Bump" is from *Notes from Underground* by Fyodor Dostoyevsky.

Text copyright © 1982 by Barry Wallenstein
Illustrations copyright © 1982 by Lady McCrady

Library of Congress Cataloging in Publication Data
Wallenstein, Barry.
  Roller coaster kid and other poems.

  Summary: A collection of more than twenty poems with such varied themes as city life, autumn, spiders, and love.
    1. Children's poetry, American. [1. American poetry]
I. McCrady, Lady. II.Title.
PS3573.A4345R6 1982   811'.54   81-43320
ISBN 0-690-04067-9   AACR2
ISBN 0-690-04069-5 (lib. bdg.)

1 2 3 4 5 6 7 8 9 10
First Edition

To my mother and father

1/11   Spirit Words Expanding   ✕ Lady Mahrady
       Never Ending   ᔒ LVMCC XXIII, MXIXX

Why a Poem?

It could have been a melody
　　　　sung up high
　　　　　　or brought down low.

It could have been a dance
　　　　a moving sign of joy
　　　　　　kick the heels, shimmy-shake.

Or a painting
or a play
or a pie.
Could have been an argument
or the piece of paper that settled the score.

It could have been anything
other than a poem:

Spirit words
running themselves away
expanding
never ending.

Contents

Preface

A roller coaster ride! Who can ever forget the decisive moment when we moved to the head of the line and handed in our tickets—the car swayed as we stepped inside (oh, delicious advance fear), our knuckles clenched, our feet pressed hard against the floor . . . we closed our eyes and *took off.*

An amusement park was the perfect setting. Not a quiet haven of grass and trees, but a brightly lit, dusty, noisy popcorn-and-cotton candy arena, with loud, pumping music, crowds, squeals, gasps, shrieks of laughter, games, prizes, giant stuffed animals, miniature Japanese parasols, and barkers calling hoarsely, *"This* way, folks, right *this* way!"* their enthusiasm undiminished through the long summer day and into the hot night—what a marvelous contrast to our everyday school and home life.

Barry Wallenstein has a felicitous metaphor in *The Roller Coaster Kid.* To be sure, it is the title of the narrative poem that opens the book, but there is more to it than just that. The world of roller coasters and the world of poetry share a great deal. Entering a poem is not unlike embarking on a roller coaster ride. There is the same shivering anticipation combined with hesitancy (should I plunge in? Will it really be an experience I want?), and then the bold setting forth—at last, hooray, going high, let's go higher, even higher; suddenly a swoop down, then upswing and downdive faster. It's terrifying and thrilling as you feel it in your stomach, in your knees, in your fingertips. Then the dive seems to be upward and the lift downward; it's a pattern that can't be predicted, that can't be diagrammed like a matter-of-fact prose sentence. Its pattern carries its own musical rhythms along and calls out to us like the barker, "Come this way, come this way and read it *aloud!*"

The poem, like the roller coaster, offers pleasure, the supreme delight of fooling around with language, with jumping sounds, with bumping sounds—playing with and playing on words, as Barry Wallenstein does here, for instance, with "Fantastic."

And like a wonderful unexpected free ride, he includes conversational notes on his poems, notes that allow us to go behind the scenes, that help us to comprehend the poems with added understanding, but best of all, that enable us to enjoy the poems more fully.

Now, on to the roller coaster.

July 1981   EVE MERRIAM

ROLLER COASTER KID *and Other Poems*

Introduction

If someone should ask me, why read a book of poems, or this book of poems, my answer would be for pleasure—similar to the pleasure you might get listening to music or watching a dance performance. Mainly it's the unfolding action and feeling, without knowing what comes next, that makes the listener, watcher, or reader respond. In a way, poems may be seen as models of freedom—freedom from the bonds of common logic and ordinary perceptions.

The first poem in the book, "Roller Coaster Kid," is a long narrative, a poem that essentially tells a story. The second poem, "Walking," is also a narrative, though equally important as the story in it is the mood it tries to portray. Almost all of the other poems are lyrics. That is, their main characteristic is that they express emotions or feelings in a brief and rhythmical form. Song lyrics are cousins to this kind of poetry.

The spirit and theme of the poems in this collection is onward and outward. The characters in the poems go out into the country or into the city or even into the air. From a given starting point they can take off to any place in any way. This is true of the poems as well, as many of them were unplanned or have an element of improvisation.

Sometimes the mood or tone of the poems reflects very little of the incidents that sparked them. An event or idea may trigger a poem but once the trigger is pulled, the poem, like a ricocheting bullet, goes its own way. Sometimes the language rather than a fixed plot or idea gave a poem its direction. And sometimes the "I" or speaker in a poem—the invented character—determined the course the poem was to take. I had to allow the characters to have

3

an independent life—to go their own way separate from me, the author—if the poems were to have a life of their own.

Everyone reads poetry in his or her own way. No matter what anyone says, a poem means what it means to you. Of course, the authors of poetry may think they know best and offer suggestions for understanding a poem. In the section following the poems, I share my thoughts about them—how they were written, how they developed, and what finally turned out. For certain readers, not necessarily all, these discussions may be of interest. They are by no means essential to understanding or appreciating the poetry.

Roller Coaster Kid

He's been up there for five days
this oddball, this roller coaster wiz;
he's ridden 700 miles of track.

About a week ago
he appeared like a ghost
and asked if he could ride for free
after paying for the first four rides.
Now, how do you answer that?
So we agreed.

There's so many freaks around.
These thin boys with dull stares
or stars in their eyes.
I can't follow it.
They come to the shows,
they hang around.
This one too
he wasn't any different.
I figured he'd try to be a big shot
and show off with six or seven rides
to show his friends he's man and can stand the speed.

Well, he fooled us.
And now all the reporters are getting on us
and all the people are hating us.
They hate us because they imagine things
they love to make up the weirdest stories.
Yet they pay
and they watch the kid

HE MIGHT be a WONDER

SOME SORT of MYSTICAL PERSON

the ROCLER COASTER

1/11

ride the roller coaster
over and over and over and over.

He might be a wonder of some sort
some sort of mystical person
like you read about in books.
I mean, 700 miles of track is a lot of distance.
The speeds are enough to make you dizzy watching.
If you want to know the truth
I can't help liking the kid.
All things aside, he set his mind
on doing something and he's doing it.

It's a funny business
lots of oddballs
lots of hustlers.

And now this kid.
He knows he's drawing the crowds.
He knows he's a smash on the roller coaster
and he probably thinks he can make a deal.

Well, I'm no fool.
I've seen dollars
when they were dimes.
I don't make bad deals.
He got his free rides;
children bring him food at
the few slow spots.
Imagine the nerve
this kid off the street
stars in his eyes
and he wants every penny I've got.

On the other hand he is bringing 'em in
and he's a good-looking kid
sturdy and with lots of potential.
He might make good.

Imagine, if things work out
we could go on the road.
We'd make all the big cities
stay in the best hotels
share everything fifty-fifty.
There's no telling. . . .

(His face flashes by
a streaming white flash
dark cars shine against the sky.)

I can't tell anymore
for he's made no offer.
He seems to like the ride
just for the ride.
Maybe he's holding out.

Watch him.
Every time he whips by
his face changes.
I mean every time he passes by me
that smile he wears for his friends
changes to a stare at me
a stare that could drive a man crazy.

You've got to watch these kids.
Either they're weirdos or hustlers
or thieves or fairies or reds

or greens or yellows or
purple or orange or pears
or twins or monsters or
movies or television or
soda pop
soda pop
soda pop
pop pop

Walking

Walking
out of my way:
On one side roses behind stones
on the other lacy ferns extending
to and through the woods.
Down beyond the garden
I ramble
finding out all I know.

Walking
in a distracted mood
down the garden
I feel the air sprayed with lilac
and tipped by wild azaleas.

Walking
I remember another walk
a hike at dusk
where
in deep mists
a deer herd was grazing:
shades and shades of gray.
I'd hunt the deer
but not now
never now—
I've found that out!

Walking
around the final turn of flagstones
I imagine seated on a broad rock

an elf who's just discovered his feet
like a little baby three months old.
In a while he'll start walking
and like me know how to tell time
from the sun
how to make no plans
and walk a distance.

White

White is where the heat is hottest.

The desert—
when miles from home
and the address of the nearest oasis
is lost, having melted
in the pocket
of desert shorts—
                is white hot.

The glacier—
dull shine in shadow
seen through mists:
hard heels strike
to shed the snow—
ice skid to the horizon
                is white cold.

White is where the cold bites hardest.

Deception

It's mid October
The tree is alive
She's waiting for cold
growing stronger
She's waiting for frost and the end of leaves
growing stronger
She'll take the snow, shed it—
shine in ice and never break.
It's mid October and the trees are fooling us
looking, as they do, like dying and fever.

Autumn Music

The tree I look up at
has no heart
but its great spangle of leaves
plugs the sky.
My eyebeams are all
caught like kites
breathless.
So still
a poise of energy
but beneath the earth
roots like a frenzy of long hair
run out and draw in.
These veins have found themselves.

And above I know soon
the wind will set these leaves
to fluttering
and in a few weeks
reds in a fire dance
dancing in the tree.
Drums and pipes
I'll hear.

Woodsplitting

Woodsplitting
is good not only for
the physical, the psychological
the spiritual
but also
for getting the wood split.

S P L I T — from a whack of the ax
or better yet with a proper maul.
Sometimes a wedge or a shot from a sledge
will be beneficial
and get the job done.

The feel of the thwack on the wood
after the heavy heave up
and the strong swing down
and the solid log halved
falling away from itself
over and again.
    Set up
    split
    stack.

This action
can get no better shape from words
than the doing.
Nor can words take it away.

Animals in Groups

a gaggle of geese
a padding of ducks
a drift of hogs
       all take care
       take cover from the storm

a factory of men
       also batten down
       secure in the snug

there is not a storm won't pass—
       this one passes too

a clowder of cats
a siege of herons
an exaltation of larks
       all jubilee
       and carry on.

Love, Beastly Love.

CHA CHA CHA

Ant

The ant walks around
and upside down
carrying his weight ten times.

Fifty times his height the wall
he scales in three seconds—
over in a flash.

He buffets into high grasses
crashes through a dewy web
goes in a circle—heads
the wrong way—drops
the weight—picks it up
finds his path home—
hands it over:
a festival in the tunnels.

Spider's Way

What black spider
Would weave herself a veil
Were she not a widow
Man
                    gone
Lost at sea
                    ding
                    dong

Still, in the north eaves
She has web enough
For home and visitors come
There is a dead center
Where she rests
                    mourns and
                    ingests.

Coming to Town

The very sun that lights the bales
on farmers' fields
spills its gold on pavement gray
and lights the eyes of passers-by
who push and rush—
little time to wonder.

And rare birds seldom seen
stop off in parks
and nest on ledges
fifty—sixty stories over head
before they—amazed—fly south.

The weeds force up through cement.
Trees stand but three feet from traffic
blocked in concrete
breathing all those fumes
yet green in spring, yellow in fall
and casting full shadows.

Throughout the city nature—
a calm assertion—pushes through.
Stars though dim and
smudged over still point down
and the moon sends a glow
across the windows of the city.

City Eyes

You can bolt yourself indoors
and brace yourself against sudden shocks.
You can shut your eyes
but you can't shut out
the city lights
that magnetize.

On the corner
an all-night store serves
doing a midnight business.
Pale faces flash under fluorescent bulbs.
The teeth are not healthy
but who cares as mouths are shut
and eyes captivate eyes.

Farther up the street in a bar
two men keep looking at each other
from across two tables.
Either they knew each other before
and are planning something
or they are about to meet
for the last time.

You walk deeper into the city
spying the worlds of the night—
the taxi driver's hustle
is now relaxed,
the street vendors are gone,
the pinball parlors are closing.

Sailors on leave stagger to doorways.
You look about
eyes heavy and on fire
and wonder about wandering farther into the lights
or home.

The Park Beckons

In the city
the boy doesn't hear the traffic
as he jumps from his bed.
His mind is in the park—before breakfast;
his teeth are set—before brushing.
Buttoned up, bright and on time
he's out in the air
cool under the sun.

He doesn't see his reflection
glide by in the plate glass
windows of stores, banks
restaurants—only in the mirrored
side panels of a disco
does he catch the movement
of his long hair, a silver blur.

No one sees him smile
as he quickens toward the train.
The park is downtown
so underground he goes
without a map—he stares out at
the posts like flying shadows
the bulbs like stars at night.

Aboveground it's not even 11 AM;
soon his moves will be out in the open
daytripping.

The City Is a Battery

The city is a battery
all connections sizzling.
Electric in yellows, reds
and greens—on store fronts
hotels—places that flash

      EAT

              on/off

      EAT

              on/off

      EAT

              on/off

The sparks off subway wheels
flash through tunnels
miles and miles
of tunnels.

How we all fly
under the avenues
along the broad ways
the narrow ways
sharing the volts, the power to climb
toward the quick lights of the city.

the CITY is a BATTERY ⚡ ALL CONNECTIONS SIZZLING

Dressed to Last

Leaving by the elevator
arrow flashing down
he's dressed in gear you wouldn't believe:

A canteen
       in case he can't get home on time
A compass
       for emergency sightings
A fatigue jacket
       khaki pants, shirt, khaki everything
Heavy ankle boots.

It's not to war he's going
but to a friend's place
where five or six guys
will turn on the steam
& rap awhile
cover the ground of their lives
& check out the times
since last they met.
From five or six mouths
bad information passes.

He takes a hit from the canteen
and passes it on.

The City Rat

The rat frightens even
the rails underground
at 59th and Lex.

No one wants to see it
yet its speed
its hurry out of sight
chills the spine.

Close up, dead or alive
the smell will stop your breath.

Poor rat, so ugly
so full of evil promises
if fools sing your praises
I'm one
and I want to know
where have you been
and where are you going?

The Ideal Photo

next time
I'll snap the picture
before I see the scene

next time's the best time
next time's the only time

to
  catch
      up

```
FANTASTIC
       TIC
FANTASTIC
       TIC
FANTASTIC
       TIC
```

(i've got you under my skin)

The Careful Bump

I was standing around
figuring my situation
keeping to myself—outside of trouble
when this guy bumps me.

Whammo!
Hey! I say
watch it
be more careful!
Careful? he says—why I'm so careful
I don't even see you.

Then I understood my station
the casual error of a bump
chance collisions
set me up
        and
           let me down.

At Night

The night
exposes
the similitudes
of a thousand
transitory nights

(only)

this night
was dappled
with irrevocable
broken breaths

(and)

half sleeps.

In darkness
delicately
my love and I
hung a single
star.

Heartbreak

My love you are   my light   my star
but as passions soon retreat
you imitate your body's heat
and fade
and your eyes are playing cities
miles away.
My silence hides a heart in panic.
Your steps again
one after the other
determined
on the way out.

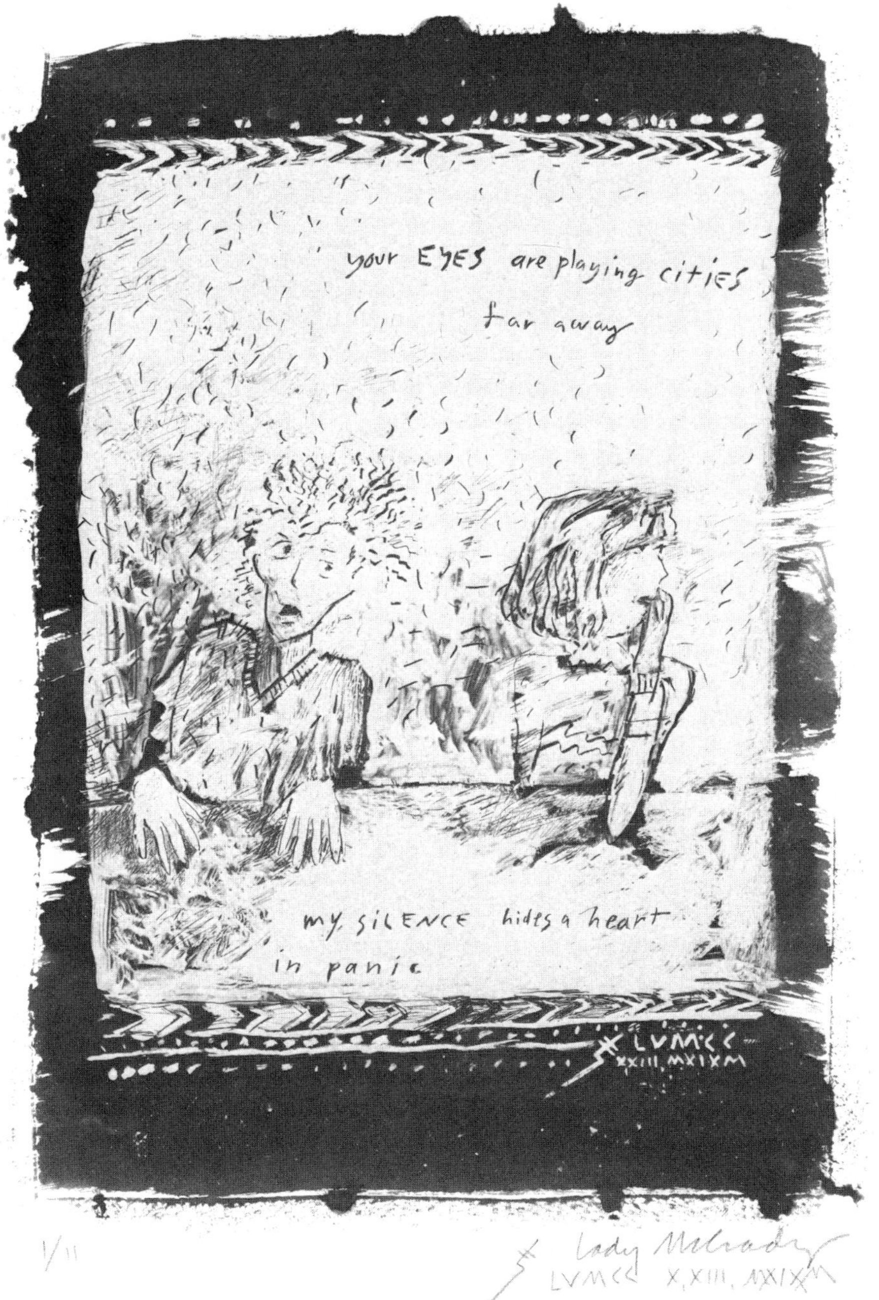

1/11

LVMCC X.XIII.MXIXM

Not the Darkness

It is not the darkness
or the roses of the darkness
or the hush of the darkness
that rests me:
Not this late hour
after a serious face—your eyes—
It is the *fact* of hours
after all the day;
the stop before sleep.

Hero's Song

There was a boiling and a broiling
in the flax of his mind
as his arms frailed backwards
as his mumble banked home
this lumberlox—lost soul
held from the start
by parents who waft him
they wrapt him in softlove
wept over his falls
his face
his future.
> Lunacy
> down to the
> gesture.

So he'd sprawl
rest back out of weary
arms akimbo
and sing out soothing
to the angels of the air.

The Wrench of Love

Cast the mind on something finer:
a permanent view
a small valley, a rise of woods
    large animals—small animals
    winged animals—creepers
    generations of creepers
    peek out, sally forth
    and bite the dust
the view hardens harboring all that flux
the woods taper up the mountains
the mountains circle all below.

The wrench of love settles
the heart's unrest dissolves.

CAST the MIND on Something FINER

the HEART'S UNREST DISSOLVES

S LVMSS

Taking Off

I used to be a was
now I am an am.
I have my being to fit to
shall I last to?
My bones are changing to fish in the blood.

When I was the sea
the storm churned
and changed my fish to gold.
Quickly my blood goes back to bones
again and again, my heart to heaven.

Notes about the Poems

Roller Coaster Kid

A few years ago, when I was driving out to Long Island very late at night, I heard a radio newscast about a boy who broke a world record at Palisades Amusement Park. He stayed on the roller coaster for five days! It sounded fantastic. Imagine this kid, a speed freak on a natural high. My first thought was to turn the car around and head for the Palisades to try to become his manager. I figured we could make a fortune—"go on the road," as the poem says.

Since I couldn't act out the fantasy, I imagined a poem instead. What materialized was not a poem about the boy on the roller coaster, but one about the man who tells the story. This person, the roller coaster attendant, watches the boy and gets lost in the speed and mystery of the feat. When working on this poem, I tried to put myself in the attendant's place—and use his accent.

The poem reveals the gap between the free or unknown spirit of the flying boy and the uptight man who does not understand what is going on, either in front of him or in his own mind. He gradually goes berserk, takes off from reality, as he is pulled mysteriously into the magnetic grasp of the boy of speed.

Walking

The act of walking for no specific purpose and to no place in particular can have a liberating effect. The speaker in this poem has a "way" or a path and here he is walking outside it. He's getting off the track. Once off he can respond to the smells and visions of nature. Everything he sees distracts him and allows him to find out all he knows. By the end, his imagination takes off and he sees the elf who points the way to a life in bloom.

White

This poem is a brief free flow of images—whims—taking off on what the color evokes. I tried to give each stanza some little turn that would take the poem beyond clichés or expected associations.

Originally the poem was a fairly random collection of thoughts and images, with little or no connection. Two of them were:

> Winter sports—
> games snow is famous for.

and

> The white whale
> made Ahab crazy—
> everything he didn't know
> was in that whiteness.

I was tempted to give each separate image or stanza a number. But during my revisions the present form was discovered, or shaped, and these two stanzas just didn't fit in.

Deception
Autumn Music

These two poems were written some years apart, yet the attitudes and themes in both are the same. There is one difference, though. The tree in "Autumn Music" is referred to as "it," whereas in "Deception" the tree is "she." I guess this happened because "Deception," the older poem, leans more on that part of the lyric tradition that has a base in mythology. In many myths female gods hide in trees, are transformed into trees, or are the powerful life spirit of trees.

The first poem concentrates exclusively on the tree; keeping the "I" out of it makes the poem more general or objective. On the other hand, the "I" in "Autumn Music" is just as much the subject of that poem as the tree itself.

Woodsplitting

Here I tried to express some of the pleasures of chopping wood, only to find out by the end of the poem that words can't really get close to feelings of pure pleasure. First came the simple recognition that words don't make it compared to the physical act and then the final idea that words don't undo or spoil the act.

What I like best in this poem is the irony of the sixth line. It's an obvious understatement, ironic because of its placement and because it doesn't seem to fit in with the rest of the list of things woodsplitting is good for.

Animals in Groups

When I began this poem I'd heard only of a gaggle of geese and that most colorful of expressions, an exaltation of larks. The thesaurus helped me find out about "padding of ducks" and the almost unbelievable "clowder of cats." The magnificence of animals in groups with their odd and arresting call names set the stage for this poem. Everything else in it is filler.

Ant

Living in the country allows me to get a little outside myself. The activity of woodsplitting is one example. Another example is when I got lost once in watching the progress of an ant.

This poem started as the record of something observed —an ant walking with the kind of great load only ants can carry. But the poem soon invented its own ant, one that does a series of things I never saw until the poem made me see them.

Spider's Way

"Spider's Way" began not as an observation, but as a game. The opening lines, "What black spider/ Would weave herself a veil/ Were she not a widow," occurred to me as a kind of word-play or riddle. The sound of the "w's" held the lines together. I also liked the punning or playing on the words "black widow," which can mean both a spider and a woman bereft. I couldn't think of what might follow, so I left the three lines alone for a long time. They seemed complete in themselves, though certainly not enough to be a poem.

Some time later, I thought of giving the poem a sentimental twist. A sentimental poem or line is one that displays too much emotion, more than is appropriate to the form or situation. Since the spider is not truly very mournful, I decided to play with the ideas of disappearance and loss. "Lost at sea" with the church bells tolling continues the tongue-in-cheek or mock-romantic tone. But the last lines establish a more serious note or meaning.

Coming to Town

I usually don't write poems on specific subjects or for purposes decided beforehand, but in this case I had just finished a group of country poems and was about to start on a group of city poems. I felt I needed a bridge between the groups and wrote this poem with that in mind. Also the idea of nature breaking through in the city appealed to me the same way as that old Duke Ellington quote: "You can take the boy out of the city, but you can't take the city out of the boy."

The rare birds referred to that "nest on ledges" of skyscrapers are peregrine falcons and were sighted in 1980 in New York City on West 57th Street.

City Eyes
The Park Beckons
The City Is a Battery
Dressed to Last

These four poems form a group in that they have a similar attitude and theme. The first is a lyric introduction to the series characterizing the pace of the city. The other three are more narrative, developing stories and action. There are the bare bones of a story in the second poem, "City Eyes," and fuller episodes with characters in "The Park Beckons" and "Dressed to Last." The people in these poems are responding to the "city [as] a battery" or a source of energy. In "City Eyes" the lights "magnetize" and draw the city dweller out. The characters in the poems take off into the city—to its parks, through its streets, to a friend's house.

The City Rat

In "The City Rat" the presence of man is almost totally overshadowed by the image of the rat. I say almost because at the end someone enters to ask the rat, "where have you been/ and where are you going?" Obviously this person has been around from the start, making general comments, but puts in the personal touch only toward the end of the poem.

I tried to escape the dull and conventional opinions about rats by expressing a point of view that is much more sympathetic. I meant this peculiar kind of sympathy to give the poem an ironic twist.

45

The Ideal Photo
FANTASTIC

These short poems are word games in the voice of a "city slicker," as is the following poem, "The Careful Bump." In "The Ideal Photo" the speaker wants to cheat time by getting the shot before he sees the scene—impossible to do, of course—but not impossible to try to do, especially in a poem. Time is the only theme here. *FANTASTIC* is a poem that is almost purely a play on words —or a little joke—if you don't mind.

The Careful Bump

Rereading Dostoyevsky's short masterpiece, *Notes from Underground,* I came upon a passage that influenced the central idea of this poem—the notion of being invisible. Perhaps the feeling is most common for those living in cities—St. Petersburg in the book, New York City in my own life. Who hasn't had the humiliating experience of not being noticed? The Dostoyevsky passage reads:

> I was standing by the billiard-table and in my ignorance blocking up the way, and he wanted to pass; he took me by the shoulders and without a word—without a warning or an explanation—moved me from where I was standing to another spot and passed by as though he had not noticed me. I could even have forgiven blows, but I absolutely could not forgive his having moved me and so completely failing to notice me.

I tried to describe this emotion in a comic situation, and although I wasn't thinking about this passage at the time, it must have impressed me when I first read it.

"The Careful Bump" was written to be heard rather than to be read. Its casualness or street-talk style was suggested by the language and phrasing of jazz musicians, and the poem is meant to be performed with jazz music. In the first version the last stanza looked like this:

> Then I understood my situation.
> I was invisible
> sneaky, a star-gazer
> a great and grave star!
> The casual error of a bump
> told me—there is a certain beauty
> in chance collisions.

This ending seemed all right, but when I read it with music the words didn't match the rhythm and tone of the first stanza. I had to simplify the lines and consequently changed the meaning. I hear the first and last stanzas as strongly rhythmical and, by contrast, the middle section as looser and more unstructured.

At Night
Heartbreak
Not the Darkness

Love poetry may be about any aspect of love or any kind of love, but usually, as in these three poems, romantic love is featured. I wrote "At Night" and "Not the Darkness" when I was sixteen or seventeen. "At Night," the older poem, is extremely romantic. The sentiments are all on the surface and by the end it is as sweet as candy. This kind of poetry, this poem, in fact, seemed very important to me at the time. There are moments when feelings come so strongly and unexpectedly that the voice of the romantic fool, someone high on love, is the only one possible. The desire to express such feelings in a more restrained voice, or through more indirect images, came later. "Not the Darkness," even though it is less sentimental, communicates similar tenderness and longing.

"Heartbreak" is more recent and is related to the blues in feeling. It is not a traditional eight-bar blues song, but has a blues manner freely adapted to poetry. Expressions such as "your eyes are playing cities / miles away" and "your steps again / . . . / on the way out" are imitations of blues sentiments.

Hero's Song

I mention word-play on and off in this book, and mean to suggest that it is an activity that is central to poetry. When some people say in a critical or mocking tone that poets "play with words," they may believe that such word-play represents an escape from reality. But many poems, through their word-play, cut into the real world, exposing it in ways that ordinary speech never could. While experimenting with words, the poet relaxes and allows the words—sometimes even made-up words—to release certain feelings and ideas. These feelings and ideas may be more serious than the sense of play that started the poem in motion.

In "Hero's Song" words are used freely—unconventionally. Their meanings are not necessarily the ones found in the dictionary, and a few of these words are not even in the dictionary. They are used to convey an impression, either because of their sound or their similarity to real words. "Flax," "lumberlox," "broiling," and "waft" are a few examples of this free usage.

I call the poem "Hero's Song" not because of its plot, but because of the spirit of the language that is the spirit of the boy, trying to break free.

The Wrench of Love

This love poem connects back to the poems on nature and country life. For me, one of the more satisfying things about rural life is its apparent stability—the "permanent view." The country seems to be unlike the constantly changing city and unlike love, with its sudden and often unexpected flip-flops. The "permanent view," of course, harbors the wild "flux" of animal and plant life, yet the flux is part of nature's pattern. Compared to this ordered life, love is a "wrench"—a whiplash. For the speaker in this poem nature acts as a balm and distracts the heart that had been wrenched by love.

Taking Off

"Taking off" is generally associated with air travel, but the poet can take off and go a lot farther than a jet. Young children, who are natural poets, can travel great distances with their imaginations. Some teachers of poetry suggest that their students use the pattern "I used to be a . . . / But now I am a . . . " in order to release the imagination. This formula, like a magic spell, almost always works because it provides a definite rhythm—and anyone can think of a change from one state to another.

The first two lines of "Taking Off" make as little sense as possible—I didn't want to hold myself down to logic. As in many children's poems where I admire the sense of freedom and fun, I wanted to set free my words and images. I took off and added the first thought that came to mind—in a sort of free association. I was guided only by my feelings and the rhythm of the poem. So the meaning here is relatively unimportant.